Gay Romance

A Romance Novel Featuring Gay Characters Who Are Male Werewolves With The Ability To Shift And Become Pregnant

(Paranormal Shifter Romance In The MM Genre)

Dustin MacNeil

Tanner had to concede that Van was quite the grizzly. The lovely golden color of his fur caught the streetlight. He was almost as huge as a polar bear, bigger than any black bear Tanner had ever seen. With their paws providing far better traction than human feet, they moved swiftly through the snow, and as Tanner had to leave his boots behind with his bike, they also remained warmer. He only prayed that their traces would be hidden by enough snowfall before dawn. A bear passing near significant dog traces can draw some attention. They didn't require the locals' inquisitive questions.

Even though he was too far away to see the driveway when the Hummer turned in, he had a good sense of which house it had gone to. The dead-end sign was approximately halfway down the block where the tail lights had gone. Tanner took the lead as they moved towards that location. He followed a more recent set of tire tracks to the house in the center of the block. The whole front yard was illuminated by a large industrial porch light, one of many lights that were on. They could hardly approach the home from the front without being noticed because of it. The backyard had similar lighting, based on the appearance of the glow between the side fence's slats.

Tanner gave Van a shoulder bump and turned him in the direction of a row of bushes that divided the neighbor's yard from the street. The neighbor's house was dark, in contrast to the one where the tracks led. Walking down the bushes, Tanner looked for a little opening into which he could slide. Because Tanner had used a space that was hardly wide enough for him to fit through and Van was a little bigger, Van's journey through the bushes wasn't as silent. Tanner eased farther into the yard when no motion-activated lights came on. He walked gently around the home, appreciating how the snow naturally muffled sounds. He moved to the side near the house where the tire tracks ended and sat down in the snow to listen as he could tell that no one was inside.

When Tanner stopped, Van sat down beside him, having followed him from behind.

There was a boisterous debate among the raised voices. Tanner could hear most of the words being yelled and those that were uttered at a normal volume, but it required some focus. It was clear from little he'd missed of the talk that one of the men in the house wasn't happy about Tanner killing the man. It appears that he was questioning the one who had abducted Parker, among the others.

Another man started yelling nearby. "Hey, what happened to you? Asshat! Roger, come on up!

Tanner tensed up and turned to face the two windows that let in light from the upper story. The curtains were closed, but he could occasionally make out the outline of a man rushing around, possibly in an attempt to capture a bug or a hummingbird.

Tanner began running towards the front of the house to enter through one of the picture windows he had noticed from the street, realizing they had to move quickly while the men inside were preoccupied. He turned to look at the home a few feet behind him when he heard the sound of claws digging into wood. Van was working his way up the wall.

Tanner alerted Van to the bear's approach to the roof with a roar. Van gave him a quick glance, then shook his head as if he were diving into the other house from above. In general, the strategy seemed sound, especially if they could coordinate their assault on the mansion. They could have a chance if Van could break through the large bay window and hit the window of the room Parker was in at the same moment Tanner did. Unless there were extra humans in the house that they were unaware of, three humans against two shifters was a decent match.

Tanner quickly drew something in the snow as Van was staring in his direction. When laid out like that, it seems like a scheme Wile E.

Coyote would devise. Tanner, though, was pretty convinced it would work.

Van nodded to him.

Turning, Tanner headed for the road. He leaped the hedge rather than going through it, skidding a little on the wet pavement. He made a break for Parker's residence. He ran through the garden and onto the porch, not caring that there were lights on in the garden. As soon as he stepped onto the porch, the siren went off, almost causing him to stumble. That was not what he had anticipated. However, he was devoted to the large bay window. Tanner closed his eyes and smashed through it. His powerful assault broke the window, sending glass flying everywhere.

He tumbled around on the wooden floor. He was pierced by

glass from the window, but his fur was thick enough that the splinters didn't pierce his skin too deeply. He stood upright in time to see a man bolt from the doorway into what appeared to be a kitchen. Tanner growled loudly and launched himself at the man. His target spun around and attempted to return to the kitchen, but Tanner struck him in the shoulder, knocking him back into the opening he had just entered. Despite his attempts to push Tanner aside, Tanner remained resolute. He yanked the man's arm out of its socket by grabbing his elbow with his teeth and jerking down. With a scream, the man fell to the ground. Tanner left him there after ripping out his throat.

The man upstairs let out violent cries, and a bear's roar joined in.

After seeing the stairs, Tanner headed in that direction, then pondered over the location of the third man. He inhaled sharply. The kitchen was heavy with the fragrance of gun grease, heavier than the subtle scent of burgers, steaks, bacon, and fried chicken. It assisted in hiding the human odors. He made his way to the stairs in order to assist Van because no one was in sight. They could locate the other man once they had Parker.

Just above his head, a bullet struck the wall. At the first landing, Tanner looked up and saw the end of a rifle vanish around the wall. He gave a growl, then a howl, thinking that the noise would make the man lose his composure. If the man was a member of the group that slaughtered his pack, he would have known enough to be using silver bullets. Thus, there was a significant possibility he would be hit if he ran up the stairs.

The man's shouts on the second floor became screams. Once more, Van roared. A large object struck the ground. There was an abrupt silence, and then there was a loud humming.

Malachai had no reason to think at the moment that he wasn't drawn to that nightclub of his own free will. Going there made sense, especially after visiting his younger brother and causing a quite protracted dry spell.

That wasn't to say he hadn't relished it; in fact, he had. Malachai enjoyed the heat, but for a while, traveling to snow-covered, chilly Canada had been enjoyable. Furthermore, knowing that their elder brother Levi felt the same way, he harbored a slight paternal feeling towards the youngster.

Despite the fact that none of them truly knew the other very well, they nevertheless had affection for one another. They were relatives, after all.

But it had become monotonous. While hanging out on a university campus was enjoyable at first, it didn't take long for it to grow stale. It needed a fair amount to keep Malachai's attention. It was Malachai's doing. Despite being almost six hundred years old, there were moments when he thought he had seen everything.

He was prepared for a different kind of fun after spending some time in dragon form deep in the mountains of British Columbia and Washington State. More specifically, he was eager to play with a handsome man when he got home, drink nice whisky, and dance.

It wasn't like he was in a rush. He had the night, after all, and as he downed more whisky than any person could have, he surveyed the mass of jostling bodies. He relished the burn as it fueled the fire within him.

The main issue was that he wasn't really sure if he should permit himself to take a human home with him. For some reason, he felt rather predatory right now. Malachai brought people home to fuck him most of the time. Even though it wasn't his favorite activity, he always had a great time, and it was wonderful birth control.

However, there were instances when he was unable to control his dragon sufficiently to make that possible. No matter how annoying it was, it was typically best for him to merely watch when the dragon was near the surface and then head home by himself.

He looked about the throng, uneasy with the realization that the dragon was very, very close to the surface. Perhaps it was the amount of time he had spent in the woods. Still, it didn't feel that way. A smell, aura, or similar phenomenon pervaded the room, impairing Malachai's ability to think clearly.

Then he noticed him.

Among the crowd of dancers, the young man ought to have been lost. He was simply another gorgeous lad from California among a sea of them. Still, Malachai could not recall seeing anything like the grace with which he moved. Not in a person, anyway.

Malachai noticed more and more beauty in him the longer he stared. The way he swayed his hips and gazed around, flirting with everyone and everything while dancing, the emerald eyes, the slender, tall, strong build.

He had the fluidity of the sea.

Malachai got up and walked towards the man with sea-green eyes and dark hair streaked with the sun without realizing he was doing so. He advanced towards him, and upon whispering to the individuals surrounding him to make space, they obliged.

Abruptly, the young man looked up, and their gazes locked. Malachai had always believed that the stories in literature he had read about the world stopping when two lovers first laid eyes on each other were complete fiction.

The world truly seemed to stop still back then, so he learned better. Alternatively, it seemed to merely vanish into thin air, leaving him and this stunning young man as the only things that mattered.

The man with brown hair extended his hand to Malachai without uttering a word. Though it was drenched from dancing, Malachai accepted it without a second thought. With his hold on it, he drew the attractive man next to him and put his arms around him too tightly.

It seemed appropriate. They seemed to belong that way. The person experienced it as well. The young man gasped in shock at first, but then he buried his face in Malachai's shoulder and took a deep breath.

It was a dance, sure, but it was so much more than that as they moved in unison. In any case, that's how it felt as if it were nothing more than the union of two halves of one whole.

Malachai muttered, "I'm taking you home with me tonight, beautiful," and he knew the human would hear him despite the pounding dance music.

It was lovely when the man laughed. He was everything. Everything.

He teased back, "Unless I take you home," and moved his hands down brazenly to cup Malachai's ass and draw him in close.

Malachai groaned a little softly. Yes, having this man in charge was safer and better. All he could think to do was take this man, no matter what. Accept him as your own, own him, own him.

Never before had his dragon been so noisy. It's not about a person. It could signify something for which he wasn't sure he was prepared, so it was kind of scary.

That was actually pretty much what it had to mean, wasn't it?

"Go ahead, please. Come on, let's go. That's when Malachai fully revealed his personality. People discovered they were powerless to resist. Most people.With just one exclusion.Malachai decided to give his wild theory a small test. "Right now."

Malachai had no reason to think at the moment that he wasn't drawn to that nightclub of his own free will. Going there made sense, especially after visiting his younger brother and causing a quite protracted dry spell.

That wasn't to say he hadn't relished it; in fact, he had. Malachai enjoyed the heat, but for a while, traveling to snow-covered, chilly Canada had been enjoyable. Furthermore, knowing that their elder brother Levi felt the same way, he harbored a slight paternal feeling towards the youngster. Despite the fact that none of them truly knew the other very well, they nevertheless had affection for one another. They were relatives, after all.

But it had become monotonous. While hanging out on a university campus was enjoyable at first, it didn't take long for it to grow stale. It needed a fair amount to keep Malachai's attention. It was Malachai's doing. Despite being almost six hundred years old, there were moments when he thought he had seen everything.

He was prepared for a different kind of fun after spending some time in dragon form deep in the mountains of British Columbia and Washington State. More specifically, he was eager to play with a handsome man when he got home, drink nice whisky, and dance.

It wasn't like he was in a rush. He had the night, after all, and as he downed more whisky than any person could have, he surveyed the mass of jostling bodies. He relished the burn as it fueled the fire within him.

The main issue was that he wasn't really sure if he should permit himself to take a human home with him. For some reason, he felt rather predatory right now. Malachai brought people home to fuck him most of the time. Even though it wasn't his favorite activity, he always had a great time, and it was wonderful birth control.

However, there were instances when he was unable to control his dragon sufficiently to make that possible. No matter how annoying it was, it was typically best for him to merely watch when the dragon was near the surface and then head home by himself.

He looked about the throng, uneasy with the realization that the dragon was very, very close to the surface. Perhaps it was the amount of time he had spent in the woods. Still, it didn't feel that way. A smell, aura, or similar phenomenon pervaded the room, impairing Malachai's ability to think clearly.

Then he noticed him.

Among the crowd of dancers, the young man ought to have been lost. He was simply another gorgeous lad from California among a sea of them. Still, Malachai could not recall seeing anything like the grace with which he moved. Not in a person, anyway.

Malachai noticed more and more beauty in him the longer he

stared. The way he swayed his hips and gazed around, flirting with everyone and everything while dancing, the emerald eyes, the slender, tall, strong build.

He had the fluidity of the sea.

Malachai got up and walked towards the man with sea-green eyes and dark hair streaked with the sun without realizing he was doing so. He advanced towards him, and upon whispering to the individuals surrounding him to make space, they obliged.

Abruptly, the young man looked up, and their gazes locked. Malachai had always believed that the stories in literature he had read about the world stopping when two lovers first laid eyes on each other were complete fiction.

The world truly seemed to stop still back then, so he learned better. Alternatively, it seemed to merely vanish into thin air, leaving him and this stunning young man as the only things that mattered.

The man with brown hair extended his hand to Malachai without uttering a word. Though it was drenched from dancing, Malachai accepted it without a second thought. With his hold on it, he drew the attractive man next to him and put his arms around him too tightly.

It seemed appropriate. They seemed to belong that way. The person experienced it as well. The young man gasped in shock at first, but then he buried his face in Malachai's shoulder and took a deep breath.

It was a dance, sure, but it was so much more than that as they moved in unison. In any case, that's how it felt as if it were nothing more than the union of two halves of one whole.

Malachai muttered, "I'm taking you home with me tonight, beautiful," and he knew the human would hear him despite the pounding dance music.

It was lovely when the man laughed. He was everything. Everything.

He teased back, "Unless I take you home," and moved his hands down brazenly to cup Malachai's ass and draw him in close.

Malachai groaned a little softly. Yes, having this man in charge was safer and better. All he could think to do was take this man, no matter what. Accept him as your own, own him, own him.

Never before had his dragon been so noisy. It's not about a person. It could signify something for which he wasn't sure he was prepared, so it was kind of scary. That was actually pretty much what it had to mean, wasn't it?

"Go ahead, please. Come on, let's go. That's when Malachai fully revealed his personality. People discovered they were powerless to resist. Most people.With just one exclusion.Malachai decided to give his wild theory a small test. "Right now."

In the celestial realm, everything moved slowly and in a systematic manner, even the quick depletion of money. Everything in Heshbon was excruciatingly pricey, and I ran out of gold coins pretty quickly.

The rigid hierarchical structure in the heavenly realms inadvertently created boundaries between the various ranks of divine beings, even though there were no physical barriers separating the different regions. There were clear distinctions between our lifestyles even though we shared the same home in Heshbon as the six- and four-winged angels. For example, angels differed in size and clothing because of the amount of wings they possessed. Wing sleeves were the openings in clothing set aside for the wings; these would adjust to fit the wings when they were folded. Wing protectors, sometimes known as metallic or lacy edges, were occasionally used to embellish the wing sleeves. Lower-ranking angels typically wore empty wing sleeves since wing protectors were costly. As a result, when they went shopping, lower-ranking angels' clothing was typically shown in sparsely furnished storefronts, much like in a human store. Conversely, the most opulent shops frequently featured the attire of angels of higher rank, showcasing their wing protectors in all of theirsplendor. Equal to the separation between angels, lesser angels would never set foot in such establishments. They knew they could live for a year or two with just one wing protector.

Therefore, it could be depressing to live in the same city as angels of a higher level. Carlo came to me to complain when he couldn't bear the loneliness and disregarded my reasons for some time. He would discourse for ages about the life of the angels with six wings, and then, at some point, he would talk about his own personal misery. Normally, I would tell him to go get a job, but he would just keep whining and ignore me. I stopped interacting with him because I thought this was a bit of a waste of time. Eventually, he sought someone else to confide in after realizing I wasn't responding to him.

Despite the limited time, I made the decision to look for work in order to support myself and the fussy, ostentatious little child I suddenly had to take care of.

In Heshbon, what kind of employment could a jobless angel with no prior work experience find?

It was an off-book employment, of course.

An adult divine creature earned at least one gold coin every hour under Heshbon's policies. I managed to secure employment at the "Wings of Grace Café," a restaurant where my hourly wage was a meager three silver pennies. After every workday, there was only cash payment; there were no contracts or perks. Although it sounded a little restricting, it was also really simple.

Even the restaurant's waiters, who were in charge of delivering food, had to have at least two sets of gorgeous wings on the sixth day. I was forced to work the dishwasher in the kitchen, having just one pair of wings. I would remove the mounds of filthy dishes from the magic circle, put them on the dishwasher's conveyor belt, and then push the wash button. That was all I did for a living, thousands of times a day. Beside me at work was the chef's assistant, whose job was even more repetitive. Occasionally, when they were short-staffed

Anybody who has worked in this field long enough understands that it may drive one crazy. During her tenure at "Wings of Grace Café," the assistant broke a couple of plates by mistake in less than two weeks of employment. The manager chastised him until he eventually lost it. He lost his temper, exclaimed, "I'm done with Heshbon!" and loudly tore off his uniform. I would much prefer to return to Pano and get employment, earning six copper pennies each hour. There, I can eat healthily and sleep soundly. What makes having four wings so fantastic? You are merely the descendants of Thrones, Cherubim, and Seraphim! On the third day, I returned to be married and start a family. What doesHeshbon and Santa Filia mean to me? It's none of my dang concern if it has six or four wings. Fuck you!" He vanished from the restaurant like a shot out of a rocket, leaving no trace.

Maybe this guy went too far in his outburst, for a lot of the four-winged angels that worked in the kitchen were moved by his ferocious shout and soon departed from Heshbon to dwell in the lower regions. Another friend, his eyes full of tears, stroked my shoulder and told me he was going on an amazing tour of the Second Heaven. In a month, he will send me a postcard, he vowed.

These people's departure increased my workload. I handled everything, including delivering ingredients and cleaning and serving the food. Luckily, the boss saw my hard work and developed a conscience, increasing my pay to four silver pieces each hour. As a result, I started returning home at an increasingly late hour. Whenever I came back, Lucifinil was already sound asleep. I opened the door cautiously so as not to wake him. However, when I did open it, I discovered him sitting up at the bedside, inspecting me with a superior expression.

"Where did you go?"

"Oh, you're not asleep yet. Just went out for a drink with some friends," I stretched and yawned. Do you have a hunger pang?

Lucifinil's large blue eyes were slightly squinted as his two small, fair hands lay outside the cover. He did not respond to my query.

"It appears that you're hungry. I'll prepare a late-night snack for you."

I arranged the Jerusalem-style meal, Baked Scallop Egg, in front of him thirty minutes later. I got dressed in my pajamas and got ready for bed. Lucifinil's gaze lingered on my shoulder even though he was holding the tray. "What's that?"

I quickly looked at the area he was focusing on. A bandage covered a wound I'd picked up two days earlier inadvertently in the kitchen. Although it was a bloody scene at the moment, the bone was unaffected, and the bleeding ceased.

"At school, I had a fall. Nothing serious is wrong with it."

Lucifinil gave me a long look. "Come here, let me heal it." I got into my jammies and took a seat next to him. He tended to my wound quickly.

"Be more careful in the future." The child attempted to sound mature by lowering his voice.

As I saw him shoving scallops into his tiny mouth, I patted his head. Pain twinged in my stomach.

"Would you like some?" He took a couple of nibbles and put them in my mouth.

"I ate outside, so no need. I'm not starving.

I said this, and then I just fell asleep on the bed. But the smell of cooking permeated the space, unsettling me. Meals were not even provided while working covertly in Heshbon, where pricey ingredients might make a single meal last a long time. I never would have thought that I would get to the point where I was unable to pay for even a simple meal.

Javier murmured, his voice full of contentment and sleepiness, "I need a cigarette."

Do you smoke? Miguel enquired, taken aback. Under fresh

sheets, they were perched on the cushions, their bodies outlined by the dim glow of a little oil lamp.

"No," Javier replied with a smile, his head heaved into Miguel's armpit. "But we just did something so intense that I might have to start now."

Miguel giggled as he drew Javier in closer and gave him a kiss on his curls. He said, "I forgot how quiet it could be here," after a while.

"It seemed like there was noise of some form all day long when the girls were here. But it's silent again now that you're the only one here.

Javier said, "I like it," closing his eyes and succumbing to slumber. "At last, I hear your heartbeat."

Startled, Miguel cast a glance down at the slumbering guy leaning against him. Although he hadn't expected to feel attracted to him, he was beginning to realize that this wasn't just two attractive people hanging out for fun. He was fond of Javier. Admired him a lot. Like him, he was sweet, collected, and endowed with a golden heart. In addition, he was naturally subservient. He was a natural at following directions and would happily do so.

Miguel watched Javier sleep for the next hour, utterly exhausted, though he was too. He admired his beauty. He noticed his softness and roughness. He studied his neatly shaped nose and scraggly beard. He was a truly beautiful dude.

He was practically afraid to let go of Javier as he finally drifted off to sleep. They drifted into their dreams together. Through their unconsciousness, they clung to one another in the real world while they dreamed of one another, their fears, and their fantasies.

Nowadays, shifters hardly ever find partners, but they do in some way.

~

Like the first morning he had arrived, Javier woke up to find his bed empty. He could hear the coffee maker brewing and the sizzling bacon from the kitchen. He stretched lazily as memories of the previous night came flooding back to him, and he grinned into the pillows. It had been the most exquisite night. One more romantic than Javier could have imagined.

As soon as Javier entered the kitchen, Miguel said, "There you are," and then he laughed. Both of them had chosen to just drape a sheet around their hips in place of clothes. "I wanted to know when you were going to get up."

Are you the type of person who believes that the early bird gets the worm? Javier approached him and questioned. Miguel pulled him firmly into his chest as he turned away from the stove and opened his arms. They gave each other a big hug and a good morning kiss, and then he released Javier to go get the coffee pot.

Miguel gave a sincere response, "I think I am." Moreover, it's Saturday. Not working today. And I believed that today was a fantastic opportunity to show you something.

Javier sat back down at the table and took a big swallow of his coffee. "Is there more sex?" He enquired. "Because I need to rest for at least a few hours before we do that again."

Miguel shook his head and laughed. Not at all. Not at least not yet. One of my favorite places is there, but it takes around two hours to get there by car. But I think you'll enjoy it.

Javier said, "I could use some fresh air." In all honesty. Yes. Come on, let's go.

After an hour, both guys had taken a shower and were driving north in Miguel's ancient pickup.

"Are we going over the border?" Startled, Jávier enquired.

Miguel reassured him, "Don't worry, baby," and took out Javier's passport. "I have you covered," Neither man had any problems at the border, and they were soon on their way once more. Miguel eventually drove farther and farther into the densely forested area, where the roads changed from tarmac to gravel and finally to dirt. As they came into contact with more fertile nature, Javier felt a thrill run up his spine.

"Is this even still here?" With surprised wide eyes, Javier enquired. "Down in the heart of Texas?"

Miguel laughed and parked the truck while pausing to take in the scenery. Few individuals were aware of the existence of the Hidden Lake as a landmark. Numerous types of marine life called it home, and it was a bit of an oasis in the otherwise parched landscape. The lake's healthy greenish-blue hue indicated that the organisms living there were part of a harmonious and well-balanced ecosystem.

Miguel only remarked, "It's a gift from the gods." He leaped out of his truck's cab and crossed to the passenger side. He smiled as he held out his hand to shake Javier's. Laughing, Javier leaped down and grabbed his hand, delighted to be in Miguel's embrace once more.

What are we doing here, then? Taking a step towards the lake, he inquired. Will you be teaching me how to fish?

After taking off his shirt, Miguel said, "Something like that." It gets hotter than hell down here, and I know it better than anyone. I reasoned that it would be a good idea to take a swim, get our fur wet, and appreciate the little pleasures in life.

Javier shook his head and gestured at the placard. "No human in the water," it states.

Miguel said, laughing, "Well then," and he dropped his pants. "Thank goodness we won't be." He transformed into his other form, sprouting hair, teeth, and claws until his human form vanished completely and was replaced by a bear with big eyes, exactly like Javier. alongside a short laugh, Javier changed into his other shape and jumped into the water alongside Miguel.

DONOVAN

I was aware that not all of Dirge was as wealthy as Azure. I was aware that my mansion was bigger than any other residence in the city. Just being with Andrea served as a reminder of my good fortune, as I'd spent enough time with her.

Nothing, however, could have prepared me for what I saw, even after hearing all of the rumors and listening to many talks.

Pandora was a garbage dump. It appeared as though the structures would benefit from being set on fire. There was a continual screech from the motorcycle exhaust. Every direction you turned, there was an Alpha waiting to indulge his lusts on some hapless Omega who was strolling down the street.

It was an understatement to refer to Pandora as the slums. I could feel the sadness in the bottom of my stomach from the image.

"Well... Sir, where shall I take you?

To give me a better look at the scenery, Dirk circled the car. Every structure seems equally decaying as the next.

"I'm not sure," I replied. "Everything has the same appearance."

Maybe you ought to come back tomorrow. I don't believe visiting Pandora at night was a very smart decision.

Not at all. Andrea is accurate. I have to witness this firsthand. I'd like to know why this location is so depressing. And now I understand why. Continue to drive.

I could feel eyes on me as the automobile drove down the street. The Alphas strolling along the street couldn't have made it more plain that they had set me as their target, even if their looking wasn't quite so overt.

"Go away," I commanded.

"Mister?"

"It was heard by you. This is where you stop.

"Yes, ma'am.

Reluctantly, Dirk turned around and faced me as he backed the car up to the curb.

"Hold on here," I said. "I'll return immediately."

"Sir, I don't think leaving the car is such a good idea."

Nonsense. I'll be alright. It will just take a moment.

"I, Master Donovan—"

"Dirk. I'm capable of managing myself. These men are Alphas, just like me, even though they may reside in a different area of the city.

I tried to reassure him by smiling at him.

Older than Dirk was a Beta. The little hair he did have was white and thinning, and he was mostly bald.

He grimaced, furrows showing more prominently on his forehead.

He said, "I'll be waiting for you."

I gave him a nod before getting out of the car. I then understood that the visions of Pandora were not the end.

My nose was saturated with pheromones and exhaust. If I hadn't been so intent on finding out more about my surroundings, it would have been distracting.

I scanned the streets from top to bottom. A couple Alphas who were aimlessly eyeballing me on the sidewalks made no attempt to engage in conversation. Eventually, I found my way into the pub that Dirk had pulled up behind.

The environment was exuberant and chaotic. Men and women mixed together, predominantly Omegas with a small number of Alphas. Strong pheromones were present. It was astonishing that no one was having sex there at that same moment.

I fixed my tie, took in the situation, and then continued. There were so many eyes on me as I walked to the bar. I tried not to let it affect me.

When I approached the barman, the elderly man arched an eyebrow at me.

"Boy, are you lost?" he questioned.

"I'm not lost."

"Are you certain?"

I gave him a kind grin and replied, "Yes, I'm sure." "This is a pub, am I right?"

Yes, but...

However, what? Don't you serve people like me? I believe that this place really welcomes Alphas.

The elderly man gave me a quick once-over before nodding.

I said, "Whisky." "Two it up."

"You are aware that this isn't free."

"Do I appear as though I can't afford it?"

I extracted a gold piece from my jacket by reaching inside. I put it down on the counter, and the old man grabbed hold of it immediately. He examined the gold piece closely with squinted eyes, resembling a novice alchemist. He took the gold in his pockets after a short while.

As he was pouring me my spirits, he commented, "I get a lot of fakes." "It doesn't mean shit just because you're wearing a fancy suit."

"I comprehend. No offence intended.

He violently slapped the whisky glass in front of me. I took a sip, and the wine burnt down my throat. While standing close to the bar, the elderly man attended to a few other patrons.

I pivoted and scrutinized the surroundings. It appeared, for some reason, much more untamed than it had been moments before I entered. They were hollering and shouting at each other. It seemed as though their already savage impulses were intensified by the booze they drank.

The man who had approached me from behind went unnoticed since I was preoccupied with the sight.

He had no shirt on, his entire body covered in tattoos that ran up and down his arms.

I rarely encountered someone as tall as me. It was unnecessary for me to stoop to meet his emerald eyes. The same emerald eyes that clearly intended something from me.

"Who are you?" was the man's direct question.

"Hello," I said, grinning. "Donovan is my name. And who might you be?

"Why are you in this place?"

"Why am I in this place? Are you referring to this location as in Pandora or where I am standing?

This bar. It takes guts for someone like you to visit a location like this.

"Is that correct?"

I smirked and lifted an eyebrow. My gaze returned to the image of the bar in front of me as I took another sip of whisky and smacked my lips.

"From what I've observed, the barman doesn't appear to be having any issues with me."

"Jaguars are in their own category. Why did you choose to visit this place?

I will reveal to you. Come to an agreement. I'm allowed to come here, and you're welcome to visit any other pub in the city. You can be sure that they won't treat you differently because you are wolves. How do you feel?

The man smiled half-heartedly at me. He cleared his throat with a cough. Then he began to laugh. He laughed so hard his rusty yellow teeth showed.

I answered, "I just want to enjoy my whisky in peace." "Is there a deal here?"

Not at all. However, I can offer you a better bargain. I believe you'll enjoy it.

"Is that accurate?"

Indeed. I promise not to tear you to pieces where you stand if you leave this bar right now.

The smile vanished from his lips. The way he was staring at me should have made me nervous, but I wasn't.

"I'm afraid that another Alpha has threatened me before," I remarked.

"Hard talk." You won't benefit from wearing that elegant suit here.

"Perhaps not. However, nothing you say will be of assistance to me.

Tension was building. Even if this man were as tall as I was, I wasn't going to back down from him.

Before anything could happen, I was having a nice talk with another stranger.

"What's happening here?" asked the man.

I looked up at him.

He was unlike anyone I had ever seen in the past.

His head was covered in untidy, dark hair. There was some stubble under his chin and along his jawline. His face was fresh and flawless, with brown eyes. Still, there was a tired look in his eyes.

"Omega, mind your own business." stated the tall man.

"Why are you upsetting everyone in here? He hasn't taken any action.

"Not just yet. All jaguars do is try to take advantage of others. He doesn't seem any different to me.

"That is not possible for you to say."

"No worries," I replied. "Everything is OK."

I raised my hands to diffuse the tension.

"I'll reveal to you what." I got going.

I extracted another piece of gold by reaching into my jacket pocket.

I remarked to the Alpha, who was standing next to me, "You can have this." I just want to be left alone so I can enjoy my whisky in peace. I get to keep my drink, and you get to keep your piece of gold. Everyone wins. How would you respond?

Ryan

As he made his way to the parking lot, I observed him. Was I meant to go with him? I nervously bit my lip. Even though I knew he didn't want me, I had known he was my mate from the moment I laid eyes on him. That, too, I was convinced he knew.

However, it didn't appear like he would follow through. I should leave him alone and stop bothering him. I was aware that the alpha had the final say over whether or not to follow fate. I had nowhere to turn if he turned me down. But I was at a loss for what to do. Perhaps he would hide me and force me to live on my own. My heart ached for my infertility as I considered the possibility that he would place me in a pack where I could work for my keep and assist in cub raising. Knowing I would never be able to have children of my own, I wasn't sure if I could bear to hold another person's child.

"Hey Ryan!In this manner.Swiftly. Calling from the doorway was Brad. He was scowling. My throat was invaded by my heart.

"I apologise." I rushed through the threshold towards him, trying not to touch him.

He pointed to a dilapidated old military truck in the corner and gave me a questioning look.

"That way over there. Were you able to bring anything with you?

"No, ma'am." I hung my head. I knew I smelled, and I was filthy. But I had come this far after a lengthy journey. I had pushed through the first several days like a man, knowing that if I moved, I wouldn't be able to carry my garments. However, it was too far and had not been good. I had shifted nervously and discovered that I adored being my wolf. I had been able to snuggle up in small hollows and sleep soundly while running.

I allowed myself a sardonic smile as I turned to face the truck. Simply put, I hadn't had much luck hunting. After arriving, I had to spend a few days hiding until I was able to take some clothing off of a clothesline. I grimaced at myself. which explains why I appeared to be a bum. That was of no assistance to me in my pursuit of a partner.

I could learn how to hunt from him, perhaps. That may be a simpler way to live. As Brad cranked the engine and the driver's door banged, I snapped back to the present.

He took a quick look. "Would you please stand down until we leave town?"

"Of course." I scurried from my chair and ducked into the footwell.

He laughed. "I planned to simply bend forward. But I'll get here as soon as I can if you can continue in that manner.

I moved around until I was sitting and clasping my knees as he pulled out of the station lot. Even though there wasn't much room, I could at least position myself to prevent getting pushed around.

I took a deep breath. I was finally with Brad. along with my friend. I had no idea how long it would last, where we were heading, or what lay ahead for me. In the moment, though, I was content despite feeling a bit cold. I shuddered. The clothing I had been able to acquire was flimsy and did not block out the crisp autumn breeze.

He made a frustrated noise, and the car veered a little as he leaned across and pulled a blanket from the back seat.

"You're right here."

"I'm grateful." I took the blanket and wrapped it around my body, feeling warm and cared for all over. His concerned demeanor caught my attention as he looked straight ahead.

I fell to my knees in shame. By pursuing him, I had destroyed his life. It seems that he would assist me. However, I had ruined the life he had chosen for himself. That wasn't what a decent friend did. I ought not to have arrived.

"Mister?"

He took a quick look. "Ryan, you can now sit up in the seat. We've largely avoided the town. He stood by as I clambered back up and fastened my seatbelt.

And I'm Brad; don't address me as sir. As you are aware.

"Gratitude."

He took a seat and settled in.

"Ryan, we still have a long way to go. Ensure your comfort. In about an hour, we'll make a gas stop, and I'll grab breakfast as well.

"Gratitude." There was nothing more that sprang to mind. I tightened the blanket around my body and fixed my gaze forward.

"There are also water bottles right behind your seat." He gave me a quick glance. "Is there one you can get for me too?"

I quickly reached back, happy that I could be of assistance. "You're right here." I unfastened the cap for him, and he gave me a questioning look before disguising a smile.

"Cheers." Driving one-handed, he drank a few gulps, passed the bottle back to me, and used the back of his hand to wipe his mouth.

Alright. It will be a lengthy drive for us. Thus, you can explain to me what transpired as soon as you were assigned to Chief Fox.

I lowered my eyes. "Thinking about it is hard."

"I comprehend. However, I must know. I looked up at his kind voice.

"I understand you're upset with me."

He quickly averted his gaze. "These incidents occur."

My heart fell. He did not disguise his anger. I averted my gaze and observed the scenery beside the road as it passed by. However, that made me queasy, so I turned my head back to the taxi.

"Ryan, I'm waiting. I must know what transpired.

I shrugged and played with a ragged corner of the blanket with my fingers.

At first, everything went smoothly. Every week, the social workers came, and Chief Fox and his wife treated me quite well. At the last planning meeting, which took place after I turned eighteen, Chief said they would help me find employment and put me up for success in life, and they wanted me to stay until I was ready to move on. I responded yes when the social workers asked whether I wanted it since I didn't know what else to do. They then agreed, closed my case, and bid me farewell. I blinked fervently.

"The moment they left, everything changed. When they didn't need me to labor, they transferred me to the barn, tied me up, and waited for me to come on heat. They mentioned that I would make a great cub for them. A tear started to roll down my cheek. But I never turned up the heat. He became furious, blaming me for everything and claiming they had wasted their time and resources on a failure. I gave up. I opened some water and took a sip because I needed to regain my strength. Brad waited without saying anything.

    I inhaled deeply. I realized I had to get away. But the possibility never existed. I tried to appear weak and hopeless so they would become irresponsible. I turned to face him. "I heard them talking about the Academy reopening and sending me there, but I hadn't finished planning everything—how to get out." I focused on untangling the loose thread on the blanket that had entangled my finger.

"So, at that moment, I fled. However, I wasn't prepared. My only thought was on finding you. I observed his expression. "I have no one else to turn to."

Joel Ryan showed up at the Metro Café at precisely 3:00 p.m. He started working at the restaurant six months ago, right after graduating from the university with a degree in nursing. Joel is a member of the inland Terra Firma Wolf Shifters Pack on the eastern shore. His original parents sold him to a family who resided on the Terra Firma Pack Lands when he was merely a puppy. He has no memories of his birth family and doesn't recall being sold. When he got older, the family that had bought him told him that his birth pack prohibited parents from raising male omegas. They informed him that they did not think male omegas belonged in a respectable wolf shifters pack and that they were a freak of nature, even in the paranormal realm. The Terra Firma Pack accepts and encourages alpha and male omega mating; however, omega males were expected to work and support the pack financially until such a mating should take place. Unlike female omegas, male omegas were not given the same respect or attention. Because they married with straight alpha males, female omegas were shielded and regarded as wholesome. When a male omega was selected by an alpha, he was expected to have puppies, nurture and raise the pups, take care of his alpha's needs, and maintain his home.

"Joel, I need you to serve every table in section one this evening," his supervisor called out to him.

David just cancelled due to illness, so we will be missing one server. We also have a full schedule for tonight. I am counting on you because you are among my best. statedMr. Bouche. Joel said, "Yes sir." Now, he had about an hour before the dinner guests arrived to finish section one. Not for the first time, either David missed a hectic night due to illness. Joel, however, was not bothered by this; in fact, he was delighted that Mr. Bouche had given him charge of the busiest and most profitable area of the restaurant. It's common knowledge that the server assigned to section one consistently receives larger gratuities. All of the restaurant's tables that are near the windows are in section one. The fact that he will earn more money than anticipated for the Terra Firma

Pack would please his alpha master.

Joel worked quickly to have section one ready for his dinner guests. In his brief tenure at the bistro, he has established a reputation for being conscientious, amiable, and obliging. Customers have expressly asked to be seated in his section on multiple occasions. Although this pleased his boss, Joel could see the tension building as the evening drew in among his restaurant colleagues who were a little envious. However, anyone familiar with the definition of an omega would know that he was raised with the understanding that his purpose in life was to serve and look after others. And he performed it admirably.

***

Before heading out for dinner, the small group of Timber Ridge shifters got together in the pack house foyer. Although the group's trip to the restaurant was brief, Alpha Nash recommended that they drive one of the pack's black SUVs, which can comfortably seat six people. Tim was chosen as the group's designated driver because he chose the restaurant and organized the event. Tim responded, teasingly yet sarcastically, "Lucky me." Tim left everyone outside the restaurant and went around the block in search of a place to park. He reasoned that the cafe must be crowded because it never took him long to locate a spot.

After boarding the Metro, the group waited for the host to assign them a seat. Jonathan took a quick look around the restaurant and was struck by the vibe. He hoped the food was equally enticing. After welcoming the company, the host showed them to a table for six near the restaurant's front windows. "It seems like we are going to have a great evening," Alpha Nash murmured to his diners. "This is regarded as the bistro's best table."

With Tim on his right and Chase and Alec to his left, Jonathan took a seat. He leaned over to tell Tim that he thought his choice of restaurant was excellent. In the Metro, Jonathan felt quite warm and at ease. He could almost swear he had visited the restaurant before because of how distinctly familiar the sights, sounds, and smells were. "Tim, was this the restaurant we were at when I came to see you last?" After giving it some thought, Tim turned to face Jonathan and remarked, "I don't believe so." We ran out of time, but I wanted to bring you here. Jonathan saw his attraction to the cafe as a sign that moving to the eastern coast would fulfill his wish to relocate. With a little lean, Alec asked Jonathan how his journey was going. "Jonathan, was your trip to the eastern shore enjoyable?" Alec enthusiastically enquired. "All right, Alec, thanks for asking. It was a nice trip, but I'm tired. It took a lot of energy from me to drive and to pack and prepare. I'm glad to be here and, if it's feasible, I'm looking forward to sleeping late tomorrow morning. I'm worried that the excitement of relocating will keep me from falling asleep at all. In order to arrive with some energy, I divided the trip into two days. I spent the night in a modest motel in the village of Delmont before departing early this morning. Overall, the travel was passable, but after you pass

Pittsburgh, the Pennsylvania Turn Pike becomes somewhat daunting.

A really kind young man named Jacque approached the table as Jonathan was telling his story, introducing himself and letting him know that he would be providing the drinks for the groups that night. To start the meal, Alpha Nash stood up and requested two bottles of their finest Chardonnay.

Jonathan became disoriented in the middle of his speech. For an instant, he appeared inquiring. It felt like he was walking on a beach, and he was positive he could smell the ocean wind. The two most incredible scents that have a profound impact on him and his wolf are the scent of an ocean wind and the scent of a wolf's fur as it transforms. Jonathan asked Tim if he could smell the same things that he was. However, he didn't. A young man approached their table at that same moment and introduced himself. Greetings, this is Joel. I will be serving you this evening. Greetings from the Metro Café.

Joel, how are things going for you? I had doubts about whether we would be seated in your area this evening. stated Chase.

I had a great time fucking Mike during our sex. After one more round, we fell asleep holding each other once again.

I gave him a big blowout the next day to wake him up, and before we got ready, he returned the favor in the shower.

"So, what are we doing today?" I questioned him.

Mike used a towel to pat dry his hair and held up his phone. He remarked, "I thought we could play with someone else for a little while."

Grinder. After installing the program, he began to display me nearby singles.

I leaned over his shoulder to look at the screen of his phone and commented, "That does sound fun."

"Yeah, I thought, why not make the third person a dude since we found out we liked other men?"

He thumbed through the males, talking, but when I pointed at one, he stopped.

"How about her, then?"

Even though she was a man, she had the same level of hotness as any of the college students we had hung out with.

Mike furrowed his brow. "Really? Her?"

We do, after all, enjoy women. or we carried it out. This is the best of both worlds, however. Tits, but a great hard as well.

He finished for me, "Dick."

We chuckled and gave each other high fives. It was just impossible to express how wonderful it was to have a true bro who is also your hot as fuck sex partner.

Let's get started, Mike said.

Jessica, who preferred to be called Jesse, was a blonde possessing striking blue eyes and a luscious pair of tits. After chatting to her for only twenty minutes at a pub a block from our hotel, we felt it was a done deal.

After we returned to the room, she quickly stripped and tried to approach me. Mike pulled her panties off, exposing a wonderful set of balls that dangled out into the air and a lovely cock, and she started kissing me. Mike kept pawing at her ass as she pushed me down onto the bed and unbuttoned my trousers.

Jesse gently engulfed me in her mouth, fanning her long lashes and swirling her tongue around my shaft like an ice cream cone.

As I sighed and relished the moment, I noticed Mike lowering himself to his knees on the hotel's carpeted floor.

I moaned, "Fuck you're good at that," and relished the sensation as she kept impressing me like a true pro.

As one position led to another, I found myself sucking on Jesse's cock while she was tongue-twisting Mike's asshole. After that, I put on a condom and began to beat her tight little TS ass while she was fucking Mike.

I was the first to come, and while Jesse kept beating Mike, I rolled off the condom and gave my sperm to him.

We traded places once more, and the next thing I knew I was lying on the bed with Jesse slithering her big, juicy cock down my mouth and Mike banging on my butt with his bare cock.

"Asshole!" Her cock twitched a couple more times before Jesse let out a cry and burst, filling my mouth with her hot, juicy sperm.

I groaned around her cock as she withdrew it from me. Apparently, Mike lost it when he saw me taking her load, for he swiftly tore his cock out of my puckered asshole and came all over my chest.

He murmured, rolling off the bed, "Damn."

With a giggle, Jesse bent over and licked my stomach, taking up his load. Even though I had just had an amazing orgasm, there was something about watching her hot pink tongue swallow it up that made my cock twitch.

With a lick of her lips, Jesse said, "My god, he tastes amazing."

I said, "Oh, I know," and she moved in to give me a kiss while putting a tiny bit of his seed in my mouth. His and her fluids mingled in our mouths, creating an intensely sensual experience.

After showering, the three of us got back in the bed and proceeded to blow each other like a snake consuming its own tail. Mike sucked on Jesse's thick cock after I took him in my mouth and she took me in hers.

It took some time, but eventually we arrived practically simultaneously, and we all ate the loads.

Jesse left later, and we took another shower. We went to sleep soon after that, but when we woke up the next morning, we knew what we wanted to do. Return to the app now.

It was Toby, a stunning black man, that night. He had the physique of a fucking football player and was a body builder. He was dressed in well-fitting designer trousers, black loafers, and a tight black T-shirt. After a single whisky shot, he greeted us in our hotel room and we immediately got down to work.

His hands were rubbing together as he uttered, "I can't wait to fuck both of your little white boy asses."

We both got along well with his dominance. He and I immediately undressed, and I knew that my eyes and Mike's got huge.

I had never seen a dick as huge and thick as Toby's; it was at least ten inches long.

He quickly became irritated and threw us both onto the bed after we got on our knees and jointly sucked on his enormous cock.

He pointed at me and said, "I want him first." "While I take his tight little sissy ass, go around and fuck his face."

That's precisely what they did.

While Toby carefully inserted his enormous cock into my constricted asshole, Mike gave me a strong and quick facial fuck.

He began to pound me with his large black cock, and I was so overcome by the sensation that I saw stars.

I muttered, "Fuck," around Mike's dick, but no one seemed to get it.

I swallowed all of Mike's juices after he exploded, but Toby wasn't done and continued to fuck my ass.

"You too," he said, motioning for Mike to crawl onto the bed with me.

After Mike followed instructions, Toby quickly withdrew out of my ass and effortlessly inserted his large cock into Mike's butt.

For a few quick moments, he gave him a hard and fast fuck, and I could see it on his face that he was going to come.

Mike gagged as I began to face fuck him after I swiftly rolled over and inserted my hard cock into his mouth.

When Toby released his hold on Mike's posterior, his enormous load burst all over Mike's back.

"I understand. It's not unusual to be having trouble with it. Things are considerably different at college, particularly when it comes to dating and finding the right companion. Around this period, you start to believe that you will meet your soul partner.

His eyes grew wide as he probably thought something that he was not allowed to speak at that moment without looking strange. To be quite honest, my job at the moment was to patrol the campus and keep an eye out for anything that needed my attention, but for some reason, I didn't want to leave Nokon.

Even though I knew that this was all about how adorable and wonderful he was, I couldn't help but squint at every inch of his body as if I were hoping to see him in his pants and swooning beneath me.

What the hell was going on with me, dear? Remember that I was ten years his senior, so anything would be strange between us. Not to add that he would undoubtedly feel uncomfortable and wish he had never gotten associated with me if he ever found himself in the kind of setting where I was from. Furthermore, because of our disparate power relations, I didn't want to feel like I was taking advantage of him.

"Yes, I am aware. I haven't even started to consider the possible identity of my fated mate. Sincerely, I don't believe he is a student here at this college. He may be anywhere in the globe because there are so many people in it. The more I consider it, the more I come to the conclusion that my potential fated partner is most likely somewhere I can't even get to.

"You don't have to think about it that way," I reasoned, keeping in mind that I wouldn't know until it was too late if it ever occurred to me. I would just know when I found my true love.

"Perhaps that individual might be me," I murmured, only putting it out there as if I was trying to gauge his response. I knew I had him when his eyes grew wide, and he reddened even more than before.

"I don't believe it's you. Carwel, you're sweet and all, but we're just not meant to be together. You really are so unlike me, in my opinion. You work here as a guard, and I assume that you will stay here for the foreseeable future. Meanwhile, I'll probably find myself employed somewhere entirely different, where I may meet my soul mate.

"Well, that may be accurate, but..." I said, "so, going back to what you said about needing help with a certain maths problem...," after taking a big breath and realising that his leg was growing closer to mine—something he was doing nothing about, much less stopping it from continuing. Would you please indicate which one it is?

His eyes widened once more, indicating to me that he didn't anticipate my asking such a question. Honestly, I wouldn't have, knowing that I shouldn't carry on communicating with him.

It was getting much harder to hide my semi now, but for the time being, there was nothing strange about that.

My body was starting to show off its fur.

Naturally, though, this Omega was also giving me some of the indicators I was searching for.

He continued to have dilated pupils. He had a feeling about me that he couldn't express—not yet, anyhow, and not without sacrificing his identity as a student at this college.

Do you believe you could assist me with this? I don't wish to upset you, but the last thing that someone would assume about you is how much maths you actually know.

In actuality, I do have some knowledge about it. You are unaware of this, and to be honest, you don't really need to, since I don't really look like it, but I have taken some previous lessons in civil engineering. That is, up until my withdrawal.

There was a brief pause during which Nokon undoubtedly wondered why I had left. I didn't anticipate that Nokon would inquire about it, though, as he was reticent and introverted.

Yes, exactly. He opened his rucksack and removed the notepad, saying, "The maths problem." Then he showed me the page on which he was struggling a little bit with the arithmetic problem.

I slapped my forehead after reading it—not because I didn't think I could solve it, but rather because it would require some time. I removed his notebook from his grasp and got up, circumnavigating a single spot. Nokon stayed where he was on the bench, staring at me and perhaps wondering just what I was doing at the moment.

With a raised hand, I said, "This is nothing to worry about. After saying, "I think I actually know how to solve this problem," I took a seat back on the bench and started to explain.

For a Calculus problem, it was actually rather simple. When I finally gave him the answer, he looked at me in awe, his eyes on the verge of tears.

"Thank you so much," he whispered, his hands quivering slightly as his leg finally touched mine. My lecturer made numerous attempts to instill that idea in me, but I was never able to understand it until you demonstrated how easy it is to understand. Actually, this is how it's done, huh.

He didn't want to discuss much about his life, but we still talked about some current events on campus, the weather, politics, and a little bit about his life as he grinned. I swept my palm over my head and said goodbye to him after that.

Nokon hurriedly walked away from me and returned to his house, waving his hand over his head. I looked at his smile and the way his eyes gleamed in the sunlight, and I saw he was having fun with me.

What was going to happen next, then? I questioned myself. Could I truly trust myself enough to try? He certainly met the criteria for someone I could love and care for as much as I did, which is to be honest about it.

We liked each other, but I didn't want to jeopardize my employment at this college, much less my membership in the biker club.

If the president and vice president found out that I was seeing a college student, they would undoubtedly throw me out of it.

Perched on a stony promontory, the overlooked an exceptionally serene body of water. Due to his father's prohibition, Drakka hardly ever travelled far or at all, therefore he hardly ever had the opportunity to take in the beauty of the planet they lived in. However, he was able to appreciate the beauty of the natural world around them—the world his father shielded him from—as he saw the sun shine off the lake's surface and felt the warmth of the breeze on his skin.

Saniyah remarked, "You're not anything like I expected."

Drakka arched an eyebrow as she turned to face him. "And you were expecting what?"

Her face began to flush as she immediately averted her gaze. "We hear a lot of stories about the Dragonborn when we're young," the woman remarked. "About how you're the reason we live underground and about the slaughter of our people."

Drakka avoided making eye contact. He declared, "I wasn't born during the Angeliym and Dragonborn wars." However, from what I gather, your people had to go underground in order to survive.

He stroked his hair and remained silent for a brief while. Saniyah gave him another glance but remained silent as if she was happy to wait him out. At last, he looked her in the eyes and smiled, a small, regretful grin.

Speaking gently, he replied, "The histories also tell me that my people did some terrible, horrible things during the war." "However, the histories also claim that what we did to ensure our legacy and victory was justified."

His admission that the Dragonborn had massacred the Angeliym had upset her, as he had expected. And for what purpose?to assert control over a world that was never theirs. But she astonished him when she said anything.

"During war, a lot of horrible things happen," she remarked. "On both sides. There are no hands in a war without blood on them.

For a brief while, they were both silent, lost in their own reverie. The last thing he had expected to happen that day was to be sitting above a silent, tranquil, and breathtakingly gorgeous lake with a woman who was not just lovely, but otherworldly. It was made even more bizarre by the fact that she was an Angeliym, something he'd almost completely written out of history.

With a rueful laugh, Drakka turned to face her. With a happy gleam in her eye and a blank expression on her face, the woman turned to face him.

"What's it?" she enquired. "What makes this so humorous?"

He explained, "It's just that I was told awful, terrible stories when I was a kid too." Concerning Angeliym. We were told stories about how they had massacred the Dragonborn in large numbers. I was terrified when I was younger.

Saniyah's whole face lit up with a smile. Drakka swears her skin shone as he stared at her. There was something dangerously alluring about the woman. But he couldn't resist the lure. She averted her gaze after a little period, but the spectre of her smile lingered on her lips, and Drakka had to suppress the nearly overwhelming want to reach across and plant a kiss. Reluctantly, he cleared his throat and looked away from her.

"You rising above the ground is really courageous," he remarked. It's also utterly stupid.

"It's also very important," she said firmly.

Drakka put his head back. "Explain what you mean."

With a shrug, a hint of longing passed over her expression. She began, "Some of my people—most of my people, actually—are quite content in the enormous cities they built beneath the surface."

"I assume that you're not?"

With a tiny smirk, Saniyah shook her head. "Don't get me wrong, the world below is beautiful," she replied, pointing to their surroundings. But it isn't at all like this. It is incomparable to the sensation of sunlight on my skin. The liberty of soaring through the clouds. There's a distinct aroma to the world above. Better. more unadulterated.

Drakka gave a nod. He remarked, "I think we understand

one another very well." "But I'm kept in my father's castle instead of underground—for my own protection, of course."

She said, "I assume your father would not be happy that you were out here with me." "And without your protectors."

Drakka grinned. "Not even close."

They conversed for hours on end, but it didn't feel like they had spent nearly enough time together. Not to Drakka's liking, anyway. Saniyah had a seductive aura. Charming. Even though he had gained a lot of knowledge about her, a great deal about her remained unknown. He was curious to learn more. He was in need of further information.

"It's growing darker," she stated while rising up. "I have to leave."

Desperate to force her to stay, Drakka got up. "I hope to see you once more."

She averted her gaze, a mask of indecision on her face. Drakka understood that unless he ventured into the subterranean world to locate her, he would never see her again if he did not speak up or take action. But he knew that would lead to all kinds of problems.

She added, "I frequently come to the surface to gather herbs for my healing work." Maybe we'll cross paths again soon.

Drakka did not think well of the hazy, ambiguous idea that they may meet each other again. He had to convince her. to convey to her that he merely wished to learn more about her and that she had nothing to fear from him.

He reached out, grasped her hand, and felt the universe erupt around them as their flesh collided.

Section Five

I could not shake the smell of the visitor from the back of my thoughts. It stayed, like the aroma of a bountiful lady. I quickly erased it from my mind. He was this small lord's valued counsel as well as a warrior. He'd be a useful hostage. Perhaps he could even aid in the military effort if he could swallow his pride. If he wanted his people to survive and his older brother to triumph, he would have had to as well.

His aroma wafted about me as the wind picked more speed behind us. I gave it time to sink in. I was well aware that people were not endowed with the same senses as me. In fact, I sensed more than they did, but not to the extent that they noticed. It was beyond their imagination.

The aroma made my cock stiff. Desire invaded my mind. It would take a while to climb the mountain and a while before I could use a thrall to vent my displeasure. It would be necessary for me to focus on my war.

I glanced across at the man. His gaze was piercing the back of my mind. With a nod, I turned to face front once more as a chill ran up my spine.

That's what they had called him, Erlendr. And what did his brother say in that voice? I meant to show you more of this gorgeous warrior with brown hair.

"Yngvild." For what duration?

"A march of ten days to Mount Sorrow."

Then, with the fewest breaks feasible, that is what we shall do.

Sleeping is not something we have time to spend.

Castles are the residence of kings. I've always heard that. I was mistaken to think of castles as extremely large communities. A huge building made of rock and stone was hewn into the side of the mountain, raised nearly to the level of the largest hall in our hamlet. The rock walls stood like little mountains in themselves against the snow-capped peak of the mountain and its edges that jutted up into the sky like swords. As a protective measure, the doors were narrow, allowing no more than two men to pass at a time.

I strolled beside Yngvild. She let me walk on the side of the walkway along the rock wall without saying anything. I placed my hand on it to help with my balance. The soil and trees parted beneath us as we ascended to the entrance. It appeared to whirl. I began to tremble. A hand rested on my shoulder from Yngvild.

She responded, "You cannot fall from where you are; you will grow accustomed to it."

With a dry throat, I nodded. The colours of the dawn reflected in the white granite that the castle was built upon. My gaze strayed from it to The Dragon King's back. He appeared to be nothing more than an exceptionally tall and vigorous man in the daylight. I would have more knowledge if it weren't for his change of heart throughout our conversation. I could feel the pain in my legs and feet, and I knew that Yngvild and the rest of his soldiers were also hurting, but he did not show any indications of exhaustion. Everyone had suffered during the marching days except for him. I had seen him sleep lightly, but every morning, he looked fresh faced, while the rest of us felt like a nail under a hammer. Now, who were we serving? This king, who was he?

Section Three

For a while, we just stood there and stared at one other, never really letting up or acting in any way that would be deemed inappropriate. I guess he finally had enough and took hold of me by the waist, drawing me to him until I could feel his cock running down the hairs on my nearly all shaven mound. I had a taste of the man himself first, then he would take me in one move with his knees bowed.

"Well, I'm not sure how to tell you this, but my lung capacity is incredible." I went under the water till I was face to face with the one-eyed creature before he could comprehend what I had in mind. He jerked in my hand as I gripped it, but he didn't try to escape. I sealed the shaft with a vacuum by pulling him into my lips, preventing any water from escaping.

I took that cock all the way and then all the way back out while I shifted back and forth and felt the waves of the ocean shifting about me. His hands were running over my damp hair beneath the water, and I couldn't help but wonder what he was thinking.

It wasn't required, but I heard gurgling and couldn't hear a word he was saying. I was exactly where I wanted to be, and only a fire could convince me to abandon him before I could complete the task at hand. There might have been anything else, but I was hoping it would disappear for a little while longer.

After spending roughly three minutes below the surface, I

decided to come back to the surface to gauge the response I would receive. As I emerged from behind him, I heard the sound of the water splashing. He was there to grab my face and catch me, and then he kissed me again, this time with an intensity I could not have imagined.

I have never had a blow job underwater, Lynn. I suppose I've been spending too much time with the wrong kind of folks. You don't come across someone that has your interests and physique every day, so I would be willing to spend as much time as necessary getting to know every inch of you.

"I'm happy you found it enjoyable." I didn't know his name, and at the moment, our bodies were the only things communicating. Even though his cock was still ready to go, it seemed like he wanted to repay me for what I had done for him. In doing so, he shifted his weight, causing me to stagger backward. I was floating on the water itself when he grabbed me and raised me. I was definitely staying afloat thanks to my naturally occurring flotation device, my breasts. When the sun had almost completely disappeared, his lips touched my pussy. I was certain that the pleasure he was giving me would cause me to pass out. He was covering my ass cheeks with his hands to prevent me from drowning, but I don't think it was totally necessary.

I just hope you enjoy this as much as I enjoyed what you done, Lynn. I think it's about time I put some of the finer qualities of eating pussy to good use because my girlfriend has been educating me about them. He took a slightly less frantic approach than I had anticipated, and I couldn't have agreed more. He began by blowing heated air on my clit, and the sensation of the heat definitely attracted attention. "I enjoy staring at you, and nothing appeals to me more than the female figure. Every lady has a unique set of features and variations in so many ways. I would have willingly doused myself in her perfume to smell like the woman he was with—she was my opponent.

"I'm not bringing you any complaints." I felt his tongue slide between my lips, and then he suddenly withdrew, as if he was playing a cruel joke on me that would make me never be able to look at men in the same way. I told him my name, so that's all he knew. This wasn't going to be entirely anonymous, I hope.

I could hear his deep voice. "That expression on your face is priceless, you should see it." My goal was to remain still as much as possible so that I could stay suspended in front of his face. He kissed me on the lips again and stuck his tongue inside of me, making me scream to the heavens.

"It's evident that you have more uses for your mouth than just speaking." I ran my fingertips along the water's ripples. He held me firmly in place as I pressed myself up against his face. Across the river, my hair was spread wide. Before the hunt started, I could feel the lion inside of me relishing this brief period of calm.

When I was his age, I'd gone from wanting to be with no man at all to being with a man who was most likely just a glimmer in his mother's eye.

He was forcing my thighs apart with his thumbs inside of them. I parted my lips to let his hungry, eager eyes examine me. I relished the attention and had lost touch with my true sense of momentary disengagement.

Though it was still hidden by clouds and preventing the animal inside of me from seeing the light of day, I thought I had spotted the first indication of the moon. Being with this kid was putting me at a lot of risk, but there wasn't really anything else I could do. He had presented me with a substantial snack, and I was determined to try it before leaving. His tongue was everywhere, I thought that I had his method down, but he would switch it to keep me guessing.

Before long, he was focussing his efforts on my clit, and I could feel him circle it over and over again. I tried to grasp him by the hair, but he was persistent in his approach. He finally latched onto it, but only momentarily, and enough just to make me sputter underneath the water before surfacing again. My head was on fire, and not just because of the fantastic sex I had recently endured. The lion was not exactly sedate, but it was clearly enough to keep me from doing anything that would be deemed ill-advised.

"If you continue to do that, then I will have no choice, but to cum all over that gorgeous face of yours." I was getting to that place and it wasn't going to take all that much to send me into a sexual oblivion that I probably would never want to come back from. "Oh my, oh my...oh my god." It was about then that my eyes rolled into the back of my head and stayed there for the duration of my climax. I don't know how I was able to stay afloat, but I think it had a lot to do with him keeping me there the entire time that I was thrashing out of control.

This amazing moment was by far anything better than I'd gotten from the use of my hands or some toys that I had in my collection. There was one that I called Big Ben that rivaled the piece of equipment between this man's legs. I wanted that more than anything, but I really didn't have the time to devote to a long drawn out encounter.

He stayed right with me and never stopped from the moment that I started to climax, until I was going to that place and unable to perceive anything around me, but sparkling colors. I finally came down, but it wasn't because he was letting me. He prolonged it for as long as possible, lashing at my clit with the tip of his tongue just touching the tip of my clit.

I put my feet back on to the bottom of the lake, and we stood there waist-deep in this water. My eyes were looking at him with lust and desire, and part of it came from myself, and part of it came from the animal from within.

"I can't get over the way you look in the moonlight." I'm not sure if he was saying that just because he wanted to fuck me, or if he really believed the syrup that was coming from his lips. I gave him one last kiss before I dashed away with the water splashing behind me. I grabbed my clothes from the shore.

Fred walked away from me, and just like that, it was over. Had I been dreaming? I looked at his silhouette in the light, chasing him with my eyes. I followed him to his office, but he simply said, "Go to your room. Get some sleep. You don't need to be awake right now—our plans don't involve you at this moment in time."

I backed away from his business, stalking down the halls in shock still.

What had just happened? Was it...

I rubbed my eyes, and I wasn't daydreaming. I hadn't fallen faint. No, I was awake, cognizant, and Fred, my boss, had just touched me.

Just touched me and told me that he wanted me.

Why?

Was it a threat?

Was this some sort of twisted joke?

I went to my room, coddling myself and my sheets. Rocking

myself back and forth on the edge of my bed.

Wrapping myself in blankets, I slipped myself underneath the covers and slowly went to sleep.

As the world of dreams came to me, I imagined a landscape filled with flowers, a sprawling landscape that stretched to the horizon. And in the middle of that landscape, and all of the flowers and grass, I saw children. They laughed and held hands, were running to me, through the field, straight for me.

I opened my arms to embrace them, and that's when the dream fully opened for me. It was a big, blue sky. The sun was spotted with clouds, but it didn't matter because it wasn't pouring. The kids climbed into my arms, and I held them close while rocking them back and forth, making it seem like we were all snuggled up on my bed.

These were the offspring I had conceived, my own flesh and blood.

And then it dawned on me: these were the offspring I had borne. However, I was a person! A human guy and humans were only able to procreate after mating with werewolves.

My dreamscape was suddenly filled with Fred's visage, and I felt acutely aware of him encroaching on my emotions and personal space.

I cried out to him, and I saw his face streaking the blueness like a comet in the sky. My kids vanished into the daylight, vanishing into nothingness. Subsequently, I vanished into the darkness, disappearing into a realm and era beyond my comprehension.

I extended my arms, but I was empty-handed.

I didn't see anything.

I had no significance.

With my ears ringing, I woke up. There was a roar throughout the facility when the alarm went off, and my head began to pound. Ripping the blankets as fast as I could, I yanked them off my body. I staggered off my bed, onto my knees, and straightened up, kicking the bed linens off my feet.

There was no fire, but the alarm had the sound of one. I gave it a smell.

It was an alarm for intruders.

Angola had been invaded by someone.

"Christ," I whispered as I gingerly opened the door. I reached for my Glock, arming myself, for sure. I chuckled at the thought that all I had been given in the face of machine guns and semiautomatic rifles was a little weapon for self-defense. I rounded the corner of my bedroom and cautiously stepped outside, not sure who may be there. However, I had prepared for situations similar to this numerous times, so fortunately, I was unfrightened. Anybody out there would have to confront me.

I secretly hoped that nobody frightening or dangerous would show up. Perhaps someone accidentally tripped the trigger as a joke, causing a false alarm. Some of the newest recruits to the CIA were recent college graduates who continued to joke around as though they were still in their dorm dorms. Perhaps it was one of them, and after that Fred would grow to despise people even more, send me back to my room, and I could return to my dreams with my kids and...

In the living room, there was movement. Someone definitely not human, a shadow I could not identify.

Dimness. They were not the only ones. I ducked behind the corner, retrieved my phone, and gave Fred a warning wave. Was he not there? What was happening? All I was wearing was a T-shirt and pajamas, my nightwear. I was not prepared for battle. Sturdy stuff: Sturdy equipment appeared in the shadows.

As soon as the alarm goes off, I whack it a little too hard. The alarm clock topples from the little table next to my bed and hits the floor with a thud. My cat, Miss Eleanor, leaps down from her perch on the edge of the bed to explore the wreckage of the alarm clock. She gives me a curious meow as she glances up at me. She seems like she's reprimanding me; "you've got it all wrong; knocking things down is my specialty," she might be saying. She leaps onto the nightstand and starts to paw at the water glass that is left on the surface, moving it a few inches as though to emphasize her point. She detests it when I pick her up and give her a kiss on the nose, but then I put her down on the bed. As I get ready for the day, I swing my feet over the side of the bed.

At least the day shift at the prison is preferable to the night shift. When I emerge from prison and reintegrate into society, I get to see the sun in the morning and it's still shining. Inside those gates, there truly seems to be a separate world—one that is dreary, unpleasant, and dark. It almost makes me think of my time spent in

Iraq as a guard in a maximum security jail.

I stop in front of the mirror in the restroom and gaze at myself. My hand goes straight to my unsightly, jagged scar that runs from my hairline down the side of my nose. The shrapnel struck me in the face with such power that it just missed my eye, leaving a large, jagged scar that covers half of my face. Subsequently, there was the fire. I pulled my t-shirt over my head and made myself look at the scar on my left side of the body. Deep scar tissue from severe burns covers half of my chest and my arm down to the bend of my elbow. It almost brings me back to that time when I touch it or look at it.

Suddenly, there was intense fire on our ship, and nobody had time to respond properly. Out of the eighteen guys on that boat, only five managed to escape. Each of the five has lifelong wounds on their bodies and insides. I turn away from the mirror and enter the shower because I can't go there. My problems don't come to work with me. With everyone's remorse, fear, perversion, and rage running rampant, it's already awful enough inside. I sometimes believe it to be the beast within. I have the ability to read emotions, and occasionally I can feel the depressing atmosphere as though it were my own. To add all my crap to the never-ending swirl of crap inside those walls would be too much. But I have twelve hours of relief as long as I go in there and keep all of their negative emotions apart from mine. It keeps my personal demons at bay and keeps me alert. I'm only afraid that one day, when there's an altercation between two prisoners,

I'll lose it all. Since the accident, I am unable to regulate where and when I shift. I know it used to happen during angry outbursts, but after that attack, I've only changed once, and it happened unexpectedly. I recall feeling the impulse to follow my nose wherever there may be trouble and not give up until I found it. I couldn't stop thinking about Thomas because I felt so hopeless. I want to cry just thinking about him right now. We were a unit, didn't we? My frail mind attempts in vain to bury him somewhere I'm not even aware I can go. It is difficult to recall the past. However, I am aware that from the time I was five years old until that autumn, when I joined the Navy and he left for college, we were practically daily in one other's company. And even after that, we continued to write, talk on the phone late at night, and occasionally even use Skype. However, there was that summer when I was home following basic training before receiving orders for deployment, and he had returned home following his first year of college.

I droop my head and cover it with my hands, allowing the water from my shower to trickle down my back and over my shoulders. That's just not how I wanted things to be. It has to be more for me. Before I received the orders to deploy to Iraq, a lot had been said and done, and I had been on a boat in the Persian Gulf with no communication at all with anyone back home. Even at that distance, I could sense him in some manner, and I've always believed that we became infatuated with one another. Since we were ten years old, I was aware. Though his father always wanted him to be the huge football star with a cheerleader on his arm, I never told him because he was so delicate.

I grab my towel and turn off the shower. I cannot continue to think about this. I have to enter that prison mentally prepared. There isn't enough space in those walls for me to have all of this circling around in my thoughts with the cacophony of lost souls. As I leave the house, I put on my uniform, brush my short, dark hair, take a protein bar, and fill Miss Eleanor's bowl.

As the sunlight began to beat, Daniel stopped his bike near the back of the lot and turned off the motor as the late afternoon light cast orange rays on it. He looked up, sniffing nervously, staring across the parking lot at the other bikes, mentally adding up the pack numbers.

With one hand, Tabitha unfastened the strap of her helmet as she pulled in next to him. Daniel noticed, hazily, that she swung her leg over the back of her bike, showing no signs of persistent difficulty.

Once more, he closed his eyes and attempted to spread his soul-space throughout the entire lot. The space looked almost fully formed, like a foggy film stretched over the planet in which his human form dwelt. It was even easier than before.

He sensed that most of the wolves had congregated in the cabin. He snapped his eyes wide and turned his head toward the trees when he noticed a figure at the edge of the woods. From the edge of the trees, he saw a face he recognized.

"Hey, go ahead," he murmured incoherently.

How come? She protested, "You told me to stay close."

"I'll be there promptly. He patted her shoulder in response, half-shooting her in the direction of the cabin. "You can wait for me on the porch," he said. In addition, everyone is better.

"Yeah," she hesitantly said. "No issue. I'll see you up there.

Daniel pulled off his boots and t-shirt as Tabitha made her way to the porch of the cabin. He transformed into a wolf and trotted to the edge of the trees as soon as his jeans were off. The figure moved in tandem.

Daniel's wolf approached Jace and discovered his in the soul-space.

Jace nodded and said thanks for moving. I was expecting this would be a private conversation.

How did things turn out for you? Daniel cut the line. Jace's wolf was painfully skewed to one side.

Janssen... Grant was right when he said that. That man is insane. However, that is now irrelevant. He murmured urgently, "Listen." Helmut got better. I'm not sure how or why, but you're in some serious trouble, dude.

Daniel gave a decisive nod. Just Francine, he said.

Yes, how were you informed? Man, that bitch is nuts! It's unlike anything I've ever seen.

Daniel sighed helplessly and continued, "I'm not sure what to do."

Yes, you do, Jace said with a mournful nod. You are aware. You must enter that area.

Daniel felt a great weight suddenly fall upon him, and he lowered his head thoughtfully. Although he was aware that there was no way to stop it, he also understood that if he followed this course, it would drastically alter his life.

I'm not sure if I can, Jace said quietly.

It's imperative, Daniel. If not for you...

Daniel abruptly stopped talking and raised his head. A scream escaped the porch. He galloped outside to look around.

He couldn't make out what Tabitha was shouting as she hurriedly waved her arms over her head while sprinting across the parking lot. She started to scream as he padded briskly toward her.

A loud explosion erupted from the porch. A massive blond wolf tore through the door, taking three steps to get to Tabitha. The wolf jumped, snapping at the air and brutally clawing her across her neck and shoulder as she shrieked something else. She slumped like an abandoned marionette in the lot, a gout of brilliant red blood shooting into the dust, and Daniel hardly had time to process the gesture.

Oh my goodness! His wolf let forth a soul-scream. As soon as they heard the bellow, all the wolves in the lodge surged out onto the porch.

The blonde charged at Daniel, who shot forward, met him in midair. With a noise like to concrete blocks falling off a bridge, the two enormous bodies crashed into one another. They growled and snapped, toppling over and scattering all over the parking lot.

Daniel was pinned to the ground by the blonde wolf in a matter of moments. His dark eyes flashed like steel as he snarled and growled deep in his throat. In an attempt to buy himself some time to come up with a solution, Daniel sought to slow down his heartbeat.

I mean, don't I know you? Entering the soul-space, Helmut scoffed.

Daniel discreetly scanned the soul-space, his wolf remaining perfectly silent. The pack had mostly moved and was skulking about the group, encircling the two slowly. Tabitha... She was still alive but heavily bleeding. enduring life. When Jace's wolf in the soul-space saw Daniel's relief, he glanced up in shock.

Why are you in this place? Go screw him up, Jace ordered.

Daniel's consciousness reverted to that of a wolf, and he concentrated all of his attention on the massive wolf that was watching him, full of purpose. He rolled away with almost no effort, bared his teeth, and sent forth a barrage of fierce growls and barks before standing up.

Howdy doody! Going to become more serious now? Helmut made fun of her.

Daniel charged the bigger wolf, as if in response. He sensed the group stagger backward in disbelief. Helmut reared up, unbalanced, too huge to dodge. Daniel slid under him with such ease, emerging from behind to give his rear haunch a vicious bite before turning around.

Shocked, Helmut toppled over and spun around erratically to find Daniel once more. He gave forth a senseless snap, scattering arcs of sticky slaver across the dust.

With his head down, Daniel readied himself, biding his time. Daniel made a move for his front paw as Helmut squared up once more. Helmut lifted his paw to attack, but Daniel dodged him, scurrying out the other side and taking another excruciating bite in the same spot.

With a roar of anger and hate, Helmut reared up on his hind legs and whirled around. Like he was under a spell, he growled and roared.

He delivered an order into the soul-space, "Fight me!"

Daniel brushed him off and carried on with his gambit. He used the same elegant dodge against his ungainly opponent twice more. However, Helmut changed paws on the third try, violently shackling

Daniel into the ground before pinning him with his shoulder. He lunged at Daniel's muzzle, narrowly missing but snaking his teeth around the base of Daniel's ear. Daniel gave a loud cry of pain as the teeth tore through his skin.

With wide eyes, Simon beheld the attractive man, whose fiery eyes glimmered with a restless vitality. "You're employed by Caster Grant?" stated Simon.

How impolite of me. Nigel, Nigel Bennett, is my name. My name is Mister Grant's helper. Nigel Bennett flicked out a pristine black business card and gave it to Simon with a swift snap of the wrist. He was a dapper fellow.

Alpha. Simon pondered whether Nigel qualified. Even though he was merely Grant's assistant, he exuded all the elegance and grandeur Simon had come to associate with the billionaire. He was anxious to go on a second date with a girl whose name he could not even recall a day ago. It has now been stated to him that he is no longer even human. Simon realized, "I'm a werewolf." I am a werewolf, and I am being driven to a tower owned by a billionaire.

Simon answered, "I don't understand," and put the business card in his pocket. "Why me? Why did I experience this?

Nigel merely grinned. "Because you were bitten, you turned into a shifter. It may occur more frequently than you might imagine. A large number of people who are bitten never come back to life. They just kind of vanish. They turn into wild animals that resemble the one who bit you. Some of them live in the wild and prosper in their new vocations. Some people commit suicide.

You called me unique. You mentioned omega. How come that's there?

That's the reason you're with me here. You see, we have a hierarchy of supremacy. At the top are the alphas. Next are betas. Then there are the omegas, who are invariably men. They are somewhat above alphas but also below them. Imagine a king and a queen. Even though a king may appear to be in charge, his inner workings are frequently dictated by his queen. Additionally, omegas are unique individuals, much as the women who inspire monarchs to wage battles.

"I don't understand," Simon stated firmly.

You only need to be aware of Mister Grant's intense interest in you.

"What makes me attractive to a billionaire like Caster Grant? I'm just a dude. I'm not really noteworthy.

Nigel's smile remained curled and knowing. He was silent as he looked at Simon, his head moving slightly with the car's movement. His cell phone rang just when it appeared he had come up with an explanation. Pulling it out of his inner coat pocket, he peered out the grey-tinted window.

Indeed, sir. Indeed, Mr. Grant. Now he is with me. Everything is alright. Indeed, sir. We have just now arrived. He grinned and brushed up his jacket, tucking the phone back into his pocket with ease. Alright, Simon. I would like to extend a warm greeting to you at

Grant Tower's private south entrance.

Simon peered out the window, seeing above them the massive structure that was Grant Tower. They were entering a vast nature preserve that stretched into the mountains surrounding the city, right next to the tower. Silently, like the flickering frames of a movie being projected too slowly, the forest's trees sliced in front of the window, blocking the view of the tower. As the car continued into the dark forest, the tower was soon completely out of sight.

As Simon waited, he was expecting to see an abrupt clearing with a road leading to an employee entrance, or perhaps a building in the middle of the forest that resembled one of those environmentally friendly, nature-themed establishments that seem to be popular among businesses these days. Rather, it appeared that they were merely delving farther. After veering off the main road onto a gravel and dirt path, the car rocked and came to a stop in front of a sizable natural pool that had a waterfall cascading into it from a nearby ridge. As the pool's water appeared to split open, Simon's mouth fell wide. The car turned and drove down the canal, which had emptied out into the middle of the pool to create a pathway that led straight into the waterfall. The canal was surrounded on both sides by walls six feet high with falling water. The waterfall paused for a brief moment, allowing the car to slip through into a secret cave through a gap in the tumbling torrent.

"Whoah," remarked an impressed Simon.

As lights flickered along the cave's walls, Simon realized they were actually traveling beneath the forest through a man-made tunnel. The car eventually stopped in front of a big metal door that slid to the side. After passing through, they entered a sizable garage that was stocked with a variety of opulent sports and luxury vehicles, as well as motorcycles.

Nigel clarified, "Mister Grant is a big collector of all types of vehicles." "He owns this collection privately."

The driver nodded curtly to them as the car came to a stop and opened the door.

Simon wondered why he was in this place as he took in the dozens of fancy cars that surrounded him. To him, it hardly seemed real. Although he had entered the car in search of answers, all he had discovered had raised more questions.

"I have some business to take care of. Mister Grant will be here to see you soon. Simon, it was a pleasure to meet you. Nigel bowed briefly before turning around and leaving quickly. Simon started to ask a question, but there were so many that he couldn't help but blurt out silence. Simon found himself in the garage by himself, feeling anxious as the sound of Nigel's shoes faded away.

He uttered to himself, "What the hell am I even doing here." His biggest issue up until now has been his inability to get a girl to ask him out on another date. He became a werewolf prize of sorts, unable to stop thinking about men!

With a sigh, he moved through the garage and up to a shiny new white Lamborghini Huracán. His fingers brushed against the hood. One of the wealthiest men in America, Caster Grant, will soon be introduced to me. This is his Lambo. It was always his dream to drive one.

Simon heard a low growl reverberating throughout the parking garage and looked up in surprise. He had something with him in the garage. Then he caught sight of it, and a shiver ran down his back. A massive grey wolf padded toward him, and he slid fearfully up against the car. Simon felt his heart race. He desperately searched for someone. Had it entered from the cave somehow? "Hey!" he exclaimed. "Hey!" Leave this place now! There was nothing more he could do.

The wolf abruptly stood up on its hind legs, and Simon was shocked to see how its fur shrank and its shape changed to resemble a man. A tall, buff, nude man. Simon gaped in silent amazement as the man met his intense gaze and walked silently over to a large metal cabinet. Once inside, he pulled open the cabinet to reveal a variety of pressed dress shirts and slacks.

www.ingramcontent.com/pod-product-compliance
Lightning Source LLC
Chambersburg PA
CBHW070031040426
42333CB00040B/1426